ALL THAT IS FOREVER LOST

To You from Me

ALL THAT IS FOREVER LOST

By

Will

It was a January afternoon, and the sky

strangely still that day, the clouds

an unusual colour. What made the world

react that way? A young girl, and wonderful

she was, though seemingly of no importance

to this place. Years quickly pass, and still

no answer to that question.

NORTHAW

1

Another day of intermittent rain and

sunshine finds her name on a stone, all that seems to

be left now, apart from some photographs of her

wedding day. In the church of her memorial, she

stands, a wraith in a white dress, as if already no

part of this scene. Her vows she made as she stood

at the place where she later would lie, a season

away, so soon to pass...................

And Annette, a neighbour, when asked

"Would you mind bringing the boy from school? So

sorry to impose.........a sister is

ill............wouldn't otherwise............"

"I'm not well myself", says the neighbour, "But I

will", and in less than a year, lay still herself, from

the same sickness. Yet more sermons and bells,

songs and tears in a church of much mourning for

another family.

Vicarage Close; the estate agent calls to the

vacant house. The rooms are damp, and water drips

from the light in the cloakroom, down walls so

recently tiled. In the aching bedrooms stand the

cupboards, fitted now for no

one……………..moves to the lounge, through

double doors…………silence greets the sun,

entering from the south-facing garden. The agent

takes the details he must take, and exits hurriedly to

Finchley by BMW. Upstairs, inside a door, two

items of clothing, her clothes, in an otherwise empty

room.

   This procession of ghastly days, innocence

lost; but remember

Julie and Annette, and remember what 'lost' really

means.

2

It's been so long now; so many years have
passed since Julie, my sister-in-law, died that year,
the 21st January, the events etched into my mind and
heart. I keep thinking of that day we drove back
from the hospital, seemingly not knowing that we
had seen her alive for the last time. Yet as we drove
and neared the village, my husband suddenly said
"She's gone". Stunned, I gasped and wanted to ask

him what he meant, knowing full well what it was, but all I could mutter was "Why are you saying that?". "Look at that sky", he said, pointing outwards and upwards from the car windscreen. The sky was like a painting, an impressionistic beautiful maze of unusual colours and shades, like a watercolour portrait of blue and grey and many other colours of indeterminate origin – but the dominant impression was a centrepiece of bright red shining through the softer clouds, though seemingly viewed through smoked glass.

At that moment, as illogical as it seemed, I knew he was right. And I also knew that things would never be the same again.

3

The village sits like Toytown

under a strange sky; the church, the village

green,

the trees, the fields, the pale sun.

The silent engine glides around the circle

and down into the deserted close. While

at the same time, back

in that white room, her dreaded hours

begin; the drugs they gave

in an act of mercy, intended

to send her quietly to sleep, fail,

and do not prevent her agony. And there,

in that manger, surrounded by doctors,

they hear

her death, rattling in her throat, but her

eyes are still watching, tortured, pleading,

looking from

face to face, and even the doctors are

crying now,

such sights to see, for who would be a

witness to this pain? Till finally, finally,

oh sweet merciful Jesus

she dies.

A light has gone from the World,

and the Sun falls from the Sky;

it would ease my mind to believe

that somewhere, beyond this life

where joy is a fable,

you had found peace.

but my eyes do not see you

and my World is dark and empty.

And the fields can have no meaning

the trees have nothing to tell

it would ease my mind to believe

that somewhere, beyond this life

where tears are mandatory,

we will meet again;

but I saw your face before the darkness

closed on it Forever.

4

I married him in Enfield, at Gentlemen's

row, on 10th August. It was a bright and

glorious day, and looking at the

photographs now, at first glance it seems a

happy moment in a life full of adjectives. I

wore a finely-styled organza cream dress,

and

though not traditional – I was, after all, not a

new bride nor a virgin – It was nevertheless

16

formal and in keeping with the occasion, and somewhat unusually for me, complimented by a wide-brimmed hat and white gloves. My hair had been shorn of the long waves normally flowing down my back, and now I looked designer-smart, though perhaps less poetic and free. Yet in the photographs, I see now that behind the smiles and the glamour, I was strained and under great stress, my eyes are haunted, my face tense. My new husband was resplendent in a smart striped suit – I always thought he looked so much more alive when he had to make the formal effort to dress! That's not to say that his usual attire was scruffy, he was always well-groomed, but when he was in his day-to-day garb, something of the darkness that

was so much a part of him adhered, and he

seemed more tired, slumped. His eyes were

dark, and often full of some inexplicable

hidden pain that he could not communicate,

not even to me.

That hurt, but despite the happiness and

optimism of that

day in Enfield, I somehow I always knew I

would never be able to help him. It made me

feel helpless and useless, and over the

coming years, as a reaction to that, I

withdrew from him more and

more, and he, in turn, did the same.

Yet the love between us was

always strong, and it needed to be.

This still white face, the hands like a china

doll's, she lies in the chapel of rest, and all the

make-up in the world cannot convince the eyes that

she ever lived. We must turn to the photographs for

proof of her existence; Julie at the zoo, making

faces, on holiday, just before she knew what was

deep inside. at her wedding, the joining, the

celebrations, The illusion of beginning her journey

when it was already almost over. At Christmas with

a wine glass in her hand, singing 'Save your Love'

to Bill, as he bent on one knee, and held a rose

between his teeth; but that was then, and this is

now, for here in a wooden box, the shell of her lies,

nothing like her, really, those fluid eyes forever

closed, solidified, once warm hands now cold as the

Arctic ocean, no warmth at all, at the centre of herself, just the deep eternal darkness, stretching forever and ever.

Julie was so young, so vivacious, so full of life. Despite myself, even now, I laugh when I think of her almost-vicious sense of humour, the way she could accept everyone as they were, so ready to have a laugh, the perfect antidote for my brother, who half the time, missed the fact that he was having the rise taken out of him, but to be fair, always took it in good part when the penny finally dropped.

To be honest, both of us, me in particular, thought of her as a bit common, vulgar, though we laughed at her smutty jokes, and crude way of talking sometimes. That was our fault, our pretensions of being civilised, going up in the world, we had yet to learn true humility in that way, the humbling was to come, but such deprivation and humiliation is necessary at times, to bring us all down to earth, and make us realise the true worth of things, that being seen as well-to-do in other people's eyes is, and should be, meaningless.

Most of all, she was good for Jeff. He too, often seemed crude and common, and had bad habits I could only well guess at. Yet he was intelligent and good –hearted, my brother, just had a lazy nature that couldn't be bothered making an effort most of the time. He too would have an early stark lesson in what life really has to offer in terms of a reality check.

What I think of most when I think of the days immediately before her death, is how brave she was, her only worry was for her young husband, she never once thought of the terrible pain she was suffering, though she was unluckier than most in the manner of her dying, there seemed to be nothing the Doctors could do to ease her trauma; indeed, it caused them more trauma than it did her, none of them could bear to watch her agonies, yet she never once complained, only when it became too much even for her to bear, did she ask us gently and politely if she could be left alone, to deal with where she was herself.

We left the hospital not knowing that it was the last time we would see her alive.

The bird in the cage must be fed, but the flat is so cold, so empty, as the visitors clamber up the dusty stairs and into the silent room, and there, in scattered profusion, are the clothes she wore. The reality of the chattering bird intrudes on the scene, the vacuum must still be filled with movement, seed for the dish, for the bird that is itself dying, arms and legs that wearily must pass the time of yet another day that somehow miraculously arrives, despite the devastation.

The dust gathers on the window ledges, and yesterday's food begins to go off in the kitchen. Dirty cups adorn the tired sink, packets of opened goods lie neglected on the table.

Through now, to the bedroom, and the obsolete double bed, and there in disarray, are the clothes she won't be wearing anymore.

I suppose we got back from Julie's place late, though by that stage, it was hard to tell what day it was, never mind what time. Silently, I made us a drink. It was minutes before anyone spoke. "Did you remember to post that letter to the council?" I heard somebody say, somebody that sounded vaguely like me, whoever that was. He looked at me distractedly, his eyes blank. He was back there at the flat, or with Julie. "What?" he said, maddeningly. A sharp edge to my voice, I spoke again, the tone rising an octave. "The letter to the council!" I said pointedly, annoyed with myself, knowing I was behaving badly, but unable to avoid doing it. "Oh yes", he said, his face kept blank to hide his irritation, not just at me, but at anyone

interrupting his private world. "I did it this
morning" he murmured, so low I could hardly hear
him, infuriating me further. Neither of us liked to
admit it to each other, but we were emotionally
exhausted. I didn't know what to say or do, but he
was, as usual, uplifting in everything he said,
anxious that I should be able to take something
positive from such a negative experience. Yet this
didn't entirely wash with me, for I knew what he
was thinking. His mind was down there in the
darkness with Julie. In some ways, that was where
he existed, what he understood best.

Stamping my foot, I rushed out to the kitchen,
leaving him oblivious to my frustration.

He followed me in. "Are you all right Dear?" he
said in that concerned and patient voice that made you
want to kick him. I glared back. "I'm fine" I said,

chopping carrots as if they were heads. He shrugged and

sighed, and returned to the other room, leaving me alone

with my thoughts and him with his.

   And I had my own gloom to contend with, that
business with my Father and Mother, the children's home

   – all of that weighs on you more at times like this,

and though I knew that he was seeing life as it is, I

didn't want to see it, true or not! I wanted Sun and

illusion and somewhere safe to stay, somewhere where

there was no rain.

   I did what I always do in these situations. I

made the tea and changed the beds. It was better

than thinking, or even feeling.

9

At St. Malo Avenue,

where the crowds are waiting,

the carriage arrives, a melodramatic affair,

a coach and horses all in black, the words

J-U-L-I-E made from flowers, seen through

the glass partition lining the dreaded casket

that lies inside. Emotions run high, all eyes

are on the husband, who must somehow survive

a day of prying sympathy, plucking at his private

grief.

The slow solemn caravan of cars trails

weeping through the grey-faced streets, as traffic

stops, and onlookers with their curious stares seem

to defile this sacred day. Again, to this church

where oh so soon before "Till death us do part"

she said, but now, the darkness has taken her at

her word. Once more the same crowded church,

the same man of God, then the tears, the songs,

out into the air, and the artificial world. Down

through the busy lanes and teeming streets to stage

this final drama of her life; and there, in that small

room, as the curtains begin to close, the cold

electricity whirrs, the conveyor rocks and moves;

then, with a howl of anguish from the

congregation she disappears forever from all eyes.

So soon

from light to dark,

the clock's face cracked and lost

in a maze of long grass

the streets so still,

the fields, the wind,

the silent trees.

From day to night,

the crawling child consumed by fire,

the skull burnt and burst in the sunshine,

the sky, the singing,

the soul escapes.

An appearance in life was made;

who could tell what it meant,

what was achieved?

Here and gone, the vacuum crossed,

the two sides meeting, healing the wound,

the blood vanished from the streets,

no stain remaining – Yet, untrue,

a change had taken place,

how deep, how far, questionable, variable;

no doubt of the change, possibly small,

but each ripple capable of multiple storms,

given inexhaustible co-ordinates.

You and I

ride the same Moon

under an ancient sky.

I sat on the train, opposite the woman from social services, the one with the pinched face and tight mouth. I looked at her, but she just stared straight ahead. I wanted to scream and shout, and I could feel my eyes were full of tears, but it seemed that nothing or no-one could change things, we were off to the home, my brother and sister and I, and that was that.

I wanted to ask for my mum, my dad, but in my heart I knew it was no use. They wouldn't have come anyway, even if I'd asked them. After all, they were the ones who had sent us away, who thought we were too much trouble to be bothered with. All we had been told was that our mother was ill, and our father had to work, So the four of us (my older brother had been sent to a borstal, not because he was a delinquent, but because there was no room anywhere else) had to be put into care.

My younger sister and my brother didn't seem as stressed as I was. Chris was trying to pull the seat cover off, and Jeff was placidly staring out the train window. But I felt responsible for them, willed myself to be the strong one, to not weaken, despite my anxieties. The trouble with that was, my insides seemed to be made of jelly. Yet the social worker knew none of these things that beset me, and that was how I wanted it to be. I set a steely countenance, inwardly dried my tears, and vowed never to cry for anyone again. And I rarely ever did.

Even when we lost our home.

11

The rain is pouring again, and it's time to

go. The family leave first before the furniture,

driving away without looking back at the house no

longer a home. The wallpaper, argued over for

hours, neglected now, the fireplace already cold. A

few hours of frantic activity follow, until the

rooms are left deserted, no sign of life remaining.

The fitted kitchen stand forlornly somehow,

beneath its oak beams and sunken lights, not a

scrap of food in the fridge, not a cup, nor plate to

be seen, no sound from the hidden gas boiler, the

heating closed down till the winter that follows

winter; for this house is history now, a dream, and

never real, a house of cards, not bricks; and in the

summer that follows summer, the garden will

grow by a different hand, to take a different shape,

just as the hand that closes the curtains draws

them for the final time; and there is no one now on

the winding stairs that lead to the bedrooms; then,

one last long look from each window, as the doors

are closed, and the past must be locked away.

EDMONTON

1

The rain is still falling, falling, as if it will

never end, and at Church Street, the family wait

for the remains of their home to arrive. Under this

new roof, the rooms are shabby, cheap, uncared-

for, and the furniture will never fit. Now it comes

in, miles too much of the stuff, marching with

muddy feet, riding rough-shod over every room,

the grubby carpets growing grubbier by the hour,

then hour following hour, and darkness coming, as

though it will never be done. Till finally, the last

piece squeezes in, and just as it does, the lights

fail, and outside the rain is falling, falling.

Lying in this bedroom with the gaudy

brown and yellow walls, amidst a chaos of boxes

and chairs, and god knows what else, with

Vicarage now vanished like Brigadoon, and

Christmas coming so soon, it seems as poor a

celebration as it could possibly be, and it feels like

the bottom of a deep well of hurt, but the rain

keeps falling, falling, till the clothes that touch the

skin are standing by themselves.

Sweet Oblivion, come soon,

Take us from this tired monsoon,

Take us from this weary maelstrom,

This restless whirlpool of stricken life,

Let us sleep now,

Let us drown in the deep of the oceaning

sky.

2

When we first got married, we set about

making a home, in the old house by the railway

tracks, in a poorer part of town. It's easy looking

back to make a glowing picture of the past, but the

fact is, those were the times we fought most, both of us bristling at the loss of independence, and the spectre of past marriages and children hanging over our best efforts at moving forward.

In truth, I was mainly to blame, at least for the surface ills. Annoyed at myself for letting my son go to live with his father, I somehow couldn't accept my husband's children in our lives, and generally made things as difficult as possible. That led me to feel guilty, and paradoxically, made me act more unreasonably through the anger itself. My husband's reaction was to close himself off more, something he was always natural at. A closed book at the best of times, he became like an immovable object to match my irresistible force, and at times, there was mayhem in our house.

Then, suddenly, for years we never had a

cross word. The reason was simple, I reverted to my Preston Park lesson in suppressing emotions. My husband, oblivious to all this, was merely grateful for the silence. When either party was stung or hurt, they simply retired to a safer place in silence till the perceived hurt had faded enough to allow vaguely normal communications.

Life at the railway tracks went on unabated. Then, my husband had the bright idea of applying for some credit cards. This was a strange thing for him to do, for he had never had credit in his life before, other than our mortgage, which was born out of desperation to have a place together for us and our Son. He was always a bit of a tradionalist, someone who wanted to fit in, be accepted by society as an upright citizen, when he was actually a complete misfit, a maverick.

Every job he ever had, he ended up falling out with his boss, for he hated being told what to do by anyone, not a good characteristic to have if you want to win friends, influence people, and most of all, keep a job that puts bread on the table.

I think partly it was my fault, for he wanted to please me, and knew how much outward appearances of being well-to-do meant to me, the Preston Park inheritance, I'm afraid. I had never forgotten those other children laughing at me in my poorly-fitting clothes.

Even Michael, my first husband, was heard to remark that "She was great, but she wanted chandeliers", which I suppose tells you what I was like. It's not that I was proud or vain, believe it or not. I was just so desperate not to seem poor, not to be looked at like that again, that I over-compensated like mad. Without me saying a word, my husband felt the pressure of all that, and somehow, that led to the trouble we subsequently experienced, a big black hole waiting for us, just down the road.

Yet strangely, it wasn't just the bad moves he made, a black ominous cloud hung over our heads from the moment Julie died. Then shortly after all this, we found out that another friend, Annette, a neighbour with young children, was dying too. She wasn't even forty years old. It began to seem that Julie's passing was only a beginning, an omen of some kind, a link with our destiny, a darkness that was part of our future, for at least until the time it was finished with us.

But getting to the end of it would not be simple, and Julie and Annette would never be forgotten. They live again now, in the pages of this book.

3

Another station of Annette's cross. In the

living room, she falls, and has not the strength to

rise, or even to cry, she makes a noise in her throat

like a whimpering creature, trapped in the woods,

left alone in the darkness, too hurt to move. No

one knows how to pick her up without causing

further pain, her husband is beside himself with

grief, yet still, she lives another agonising time till

her birthday, the sixteenth of December, when the

telephone inevitably rings.

Goodbye Dear Friend,

Goodbye.

The lord is my shepherd,

I shall not want,

he maketh my animal

to lie down in green fields

and leadeth me

to the still waters.

Sometimes on a day when the Summer

wearies,

I feel that I must leave you safe from harm,

hiding in a cool asylum,

for what does it mean

in the scheme of things,

when one blind neuro wanders off

to nowhere?

4

The worst part about the home was going

to school in the morning. The children from other

schools would see us, and in our Preston Park

clothes, they knew we were in care, and they would

shout and laugh and mock us all the long way along

the park and round to the school. It was like a walk

of shame, and I never will forget that feeling. Then there was the tin bath. It was bad enough normally, but one night I was made to share it with a boy, and my whole body blushed with humiliation. Even talking about it now, I come out in a sweat.

At times, lying in bed at night, I would pray that father would come and save us from all this, and one day, my prayers seemed to be answered when he came and visited. I was so excited, I partly forgot my promise to myself to hold my feelings inside so no-one again would ever see them, and I rushed up to him and put my arms round his neck and said "Daddy! Daddy! Can we go home now?" He pulled my arms from him, and frowned, then turned and left without saying a word.

5

A small church in an Essex town, away

from the traffic and the marching feet. A neat grass

entrance leads to a home-made path through the

headstones, and there, down at the bottom of a

gentle hill, through the deep green grass, almost to

the hut where the workers have their tea, beside the

growing mound of yesterday's flowers, her name

appears. 'Annette'; such a small stone of marble; and this is it, this is where she lies when not so long ago she stood by the school bus and waved her children away, solid and real as anyone is, but now, in the cold light of this day, it seems as if she has vanished into thin air, and the rain begins to fall as the visitors arrange the flowers and go, leaving behind a card wrapped in cellophane, lest to the eyes, the writing becomes blurred, unfocused, and all too soon, the words are washed away.

6

I think I was in my early teens when my

father began visiting my room late at night. Hearing

his footsteps on the stairs filled me indescribable

terror, and the sweat poured from me, all over my

body, every pore. I remember to this day that

feeling as he entered the room and stood there,

playing with himself. He didn't actually do anything

more than that, but that was enough.

My mother knew. That was the really terrible thing to contemplate. And that meant that there was no way out, no escape from this death within life. Finally, the day I turned 16, she suddenly looked at me with those incredibly cold eyes, and told me to get out. She handed me my birth certificate and there was a suitcase waiting for me in the hall. Determined not to cry, but terrified and in a panic, I rushed out, not knowing where to go.

Michael's family were really great to me that night, and from then on. Apart from anything else, I had only been going out with him a short time, and when they heard my story, without hesitation, they took me in. Looking back, I realise now how badly I treated Michael in some ways.

He wasn't a bad person at all, just very set in his ways, no ambition, and sometimes no gumption either. I picked on him for his lack of expectations and lack of effort too – he was a plumber, yet our first house was without water for months on end! All that with a young baby to look after! My indignation and rage knew no bounds, but Michael just ducked the flying pans and shrugged. I'd almost rather he had hit me, but he never did. He was apathetic to the point of impotence.

And I left him.

Even after I had long gone from Michael's life, I kept on seeing his Mother, Ida, who had been so good to me during those early difficult years with my own Mother. Ida had been more of a Mother to me than my own flesh and blood.

At first, I tried to do it in secret, thinking

my new husband would be offended, but being who he was, he guessed as much, and encouraged me openly to go and see her, to keep contact with someone who meant so much to me. He was generous and understanding like that. It was those little ways that often compensated for his dark sides, especially that air of gloom that seemed to permeate through everything surrounding him.

Then one night, I came home to him in distress. Ida had been unwell for a few weeks, with a terrible bronchial cough, and she had been taken to hospital. I wanted to go with Ida in the ambulance, but Michael's new wife, Jan, was there, and was very jealous of me, doing everything in her power to exclude me from Ida's life. She ensured that she was the one who went in the ambulance, leaving me to lock up the house.

As I watched the ambulance speed off into the darkness, I felt so upset and excluded, and concerned for Ida, even though the Doctor had only advised that she be taken to hospital as a precaution, because of her age and bad bronchial cough.

I couldn't hide my distress from my husband, and he sat me down and asked to hear the full story. What he said next took my breath away, and distressed me even more. Of course, he meant what he said to be a comfort, but at the same time, he was, as usual, opening my eyes to a central truth. He said that Jan was looking in the wrong direction, rushing off with the ambulance, that her sense of her own importance as the central figure in the drama was misplaced. My husband said what the symbols meant was that I was the gatekeeper, not just locking up the house, but locking up the past. And as usual, he was right, though I didn't welcome his words at the time.

Ida would never come home again.

7

It's time now, time to make that journey

along the desperate streets of the city, through the

gasping doors of the dirty tubes hidden deep in the

entrails. And the bowels heave one more time and

out spews a colourful mass of crazily-assorted

people, all shapes and sizes, regurgitated all over

the grimy pavement and into the clogged-up emphysematous arteries of the aching city, where one such foreign body meets with the white cells, deep in a pigeon-spattered tomb of a place, stuck on a concrete slab, like part of an 'airfix' kit. More questions, the same questions, more answers, the same answers, then a trudge to the dungeon, to rot until such time.

For now that the festering sore is lanced, the surgeons have no concern for what becomes of the boil, it can be watered and fed, cultivated like a germ, to see what it does next. Meanwhile, in the dish, the thing is shedding its skin, the old life is going, pacing up and down the floor, five steps right, three left, wearing itself out, till at last it finds relief, postponing the pain till another time in the relentless future.

8

Each time he went to face the court, my heart was in my mouth, my stomach lurching, and I know he felt the same. We clung to each other like limpets, frightened children afraid of the dark forces gathering against us. Everything we knew seemed to be falling to dust.

In his usual way, he had foreseen all this the moment Julie died, which of course, was no help whatsoever to either of us.

9

In the park behind the cemetery, Shane the

dog is running through the lanes of trees that toss

their wild hair in the wind. Sheets of rain are

sweeping across the fields, and the umbrella held

like a lance tries to turn itself inside out in this

tournament of the seasons. Yet the weather seems

distant, from another time, for the sound of the

howling wind is drowned out by the onrushing

train, and the skin is too numb to feel the stinging

rain, pouring down like the first great flood,

drowning out the memory of sweet bygone days.

How many hours are there left for such walks in

the park, and the freedom of the wind and the rain,

and the rush back through the cemetery before the

dark closes the gates? And all the way along, the

lights of the warm house that seem so full of the

cares of the unconcerned. Paradise is cancelled,

the future is not a pretty sight, now if the past

would rest in peace, but it can't be, and the

present, that butterfly, hangs transfixed between

two flames.

10

At least I did have my garden. It was my

place, a place I could lose myself, find myself, my

world. But one day, even that was taken away, and

there was no garden, nowhere for me to go. Several

times in my life this happened, and though each

time a garden came back, it was never the same one,

and in its going, each pleasure was diminished

when it returned, for nothing is ever truly replaced.

11

It is the night of the last supper. It is time
to prepare. Camelot as a concept, has ceased to be,
harsh realities must knock at the doors of this
estate. Now we must suffer the fate of all fools
who fall from grace, and cut the silken cloth to
suit, for winter has come to the green grass and
once-pleasant lawns of this place. Many a season

will now pass before a gentleness comes again to

this land, so sleep, hush, dry your tears, and

though the morning brings sorrow, rise above this.

See how a new city was made from the ruins of

Berlin; downstairs, in that small jar of water,

where you planted a cutting from the dying

Lonicera, there is a tiny shoot of green springing

into life against all the odds, all this from the

touch of your hand. So take heart, nature will not

abandon us now, as long as we continue to reach

for light.

These two warm bodies

wrapped against the cold,

two silent figures in a darkened room.

Don't say a word,

my mind has heard,

everytime you've faced yourself

with a World, absurd;

but what can I say

to take your bad dreams away?

If I could have one wish

to last me all my life

I would use it to bring you peace of mind.

12

When he said goodbye and left home that day, I was scared I would never see him again. Yet I couldn't believe that such a thing would happen. All the solicitors and barristers had insisted that he would not receive a custodial sentence, that it was merely a matter for censure, he was, after all, innocent of stealing or direct fraud, just naïve in his thinking.

But of course, what we didn't know was how

badly the authorities are upset when they come across someone they perceive as being too clever by half, especially when it comes to anything to do with money. Judges after all, are just promoted barristers, and barristers in general, are money-mad.

So, though both of us hoped for the best, we were to receive the worst. I think he, in his heart, knew that he was unlucky in such situations, and had prepared a series of letters for me to open and read for 52 weeks. It turned out he was absolutely right. But what good it did being right I have yet to understand.

BRIXTON

1

Southwark is a cold part of the city,

somehow always grey, mounds of dog shit litter

the way, and people out of Dickens choke the

dusty streets. Here, by the Thames, they have built

a new court to disguise their medieval ways.

Watchdogs wait at the modern door, and tea in the

cafeteria seems almost sane, the clatter of

waitresses, the chatter of everyday conversation;

but the black-robed barrister drowns all sound –

"Four years for this", he says, then he carries on

with the text he prepared, but his voice melts into

the background, sound of the real world fading

fast, slipping from grasp, mechanical noise, vague

customers, scene becoming blurred, closed doors,

closed doors, closed doors.

2

He did try his best to live a normal life, but he

was not a normal person. His head was always full

of stuff, stuff I didn't't understand – nor want to – it

didn't seem to give him much peace, how I wished I

could have taken some of it on board for him! But

he was so damned silent most of the time, and then

he would go the other way, and make great ranting

speeches that drove you bananas! He would march

up and down, his Scottish accent all the more aggressive for the verbal violence and use of words seemingly calculated for maximum effect. And if someone else was to interject, that would only make him worse! No matter how much anyone tried to match him, he always had to go further, go one better. He was unbeatable in his invective, in his anger, his indignation at the world around him. But it all came from his inner torment, a darkness that eclipsed my own, and it seemed to have no discernible cause. Perhaps it was just there, in his makeup, something he had carried inside all his life.

And there was no cure for it.

3

Into the valley too deaf and dumb to act,

mea culpa, mea culpa, mea culpa. The judge sits

coldly at his bench, he has seen the papers, his

mind is set, but the lines of the play must be read

aloud, before they bring the curtain down. The

barrister shakily quotes his speech, aware that his

voice is merely filling space, till finally, the judge

looks up, and gives him a chilling cobra smile,

anxious to be done with this malarkey, halting the

spluttering stuttering unignited junior brief with a

wave of his hand, and a verbal pat on the head.

Then he turns to the figure in the stocks to deliver

the words of darkness –

Gone

Finished

Over

Completed

Goodbye

Goodbye

Goodbye

Goodbye my love

Goodbye.

And before I was nothing,

I was nothing.

A blind embryo alive,

yet unaware of living,

a sleeping spaceman alone in a green void,

drifting thoughtless, floating,

unmindful of the Universal heartbeat;

till the sky split,

and the storm sweeping all the stars

into the cruel vortex,

sucked the seed from the Mother ship,

cutting the lifeline forever,

as the bewildered child breaks into sunlight

We are men within men within men
We live in Worlds within Worlds within
Worlds.

This flickering moment

finds my replacement and I

alone in a time-drenched place,

each examining the other's face.

As the bewildered child breaks into

sunlight

a midnight swimmer in the deep sea,

gasps for breath

and drowns.

4

I never told my husband this, but when I got the

news from his solicitor, I collapsed and could not

stop crying. I had determined a long time ago that

nothing would ever make me cry again, I never

thought I could cry like that, but I had never felt so

alone before. Somehow it was worse than Preston

Park and my Mother and Father, all that. For at

least then, I knew I was totally alone, and had to be hard on myself to survive. Now I had met someone who had entered my world, and been part of me, and there was the children too. In some ways, not being alone made me more alone than ever. When he vanished that day, it changed everything, nothing would ever be the same again, for either of us.

5

The bus to Brixton passes the building
society where the lights shine in the dark, and
people walk from their parked cars to window
shop in the brightness. Crossing at the Elephant
and Castle, the shadowy spectators inside the bus
are no part of this scene, they sit in the gloom of a
ghostly interior, stuck with each other, almost
hand in hand, stories to tell, sad bravado to relate,
over the last cigarette.

The young man with the earring curses and

covers his fear with anger. "Lifed off!" he shouts,
shooting his mouth like a pistol, bewildered child,
caught in this web, so unaware of the implications
of thoughtless actions, now to be seen in their
entirety, years too late. The Rasta laughs, a hyena
among the lions and the deer. "Result! Result!" –
phrases to learn to swing in this jungle, swimming
lessons with piranha, keywords, needed to pass
through one dangerous door to another.

"Sweet as a nut!" the Rasta yells, grinning
madly, and the dumbstruck novice feels like a
fool, as well as a clown and a charlatan.

The castle raised the portcullis, and knight
takes pawn through a line of black and white
photographs and prints, stamped, categorised,
staggering to a blue plastic plate scarred with
yesterdays, which now must take yet more food to

match, Sesame Street stuff, play food from a joke shop, it splats on the plate, and is consumed with disgust in every sense.

And now to the market of the robes; the fat man strips, the Romans laugh as they did in ancient times, they toss the dice, and look for a crown of thorns. All those who wait join in this game of their own mockery. Accidentally, a garment falls. "Sorry" says the fat man, unnecessarily. "You fucking will be!" is the bleak reply as rows of ridiculous robes on spindly legs shuffle through from station to station.

"Next!" says the doctor, ringing the till. "Are you ill? – No? – Next!" (Occasionally an aspirin, that should do the trick).

Midnight. Almost pathetically glad, these shabby figures fill their allotted space and slump in stunned disbelief. Instant friends and enemies meet, and must make their beds. Fritz removes the puff from his arse, and all will inhale the smoke that cures such ills if only for a time (such a little time), but first, he pauses in mid-sentence, and shits in a pot, like a naughty child, his companions pretending not to notice, as the conversation resumes.

The world is now twelve by six, and inhabited by three, two black, one white for tea. The sky and the horizon are covered in graffiti, and someone has pissed the beds. Now, ambition has shrunk to cell size, prayers for category D, but God pays no attention, nor does anyone, no one comes, there is nothing to do, nothing to see. Time sticks to the walls and will not move; although the sun rises and falls, and the rain comes and goes, they do not touch this place, deep in the earth,

with only a shaft of light reaching down from on

high, and every 24 hours the cycle repeats itself,

repeats, repeats, repeats itself.

Closed

Unmoving

Pen dipped in grey

People in locked heads

Pain shifts around but cannot escape

Somehow finally here

Sanity by a thread

Thoughts that squeeze through

Free this singing bird in the chapel

Someone's daylight in the window

Air a welcome visitor

Three travellers

Cups worn

Tired of dry mouths

Passing passing passing

Movement

Two now

Red hand grips the heart

Who can fill this space?

Door closes

End of all light

Such silent witness

Sweet flash of sacred faces

Beautiful

Terrifying

6

The first weeks went by in a daze. Painful as

they were, they were nothing compared to the

seemingly-endless days and nights that followed

when the reality and grief began to take hold. The

nights were, of course, the worst. Ever since those

ghastly nights of my Father, I always dreaded the

dark, and even going to bed, hardly ever sleeping, even though he had been dead so many years. Something like that stays with you always. And now, there was no-one there. Somehow, it made my heart harden too. I became, yet again, that automaton who survived my Father, my Mother, Preston Park, and all of that. But it meant that my soul was closed to warmth, to love, to as much feeling as possible.

As well as that, I knew him so well that I knew what he must be thinking, feeling. I had no way of knowing exactly what his experience in those awful places were, but I knew his head well enough to know that being trapped would not suit him – not that it suits anyone, such a thing, but for him, with his spirit the way it was, the experience would be multiplied in his soul. I also realised that he would take it hard knowing that from now on he would be looked upon as an outcast, a completely different species, almost inhuman. That's the price anyone pays who becomes 'one of them', a lost child of this world. I knew he was tough. I knew he would survive anything. But I knew he would come home as somebody I did not recognise anymore. That's what places like that do to people. Someone like him, who could perhaps survive the experience there as well as it was possible to do, but the price for that survival would be demons unleashed that could never be contained in the sunlight of freedom.

7

When morning arrives, the mind retreats

from the thunderous rumble of running feet with

nowhere to go; these unaccustomed sounds are

only breakfast in its new form. Then, a closed

door, till exercise, a term that means using legs.

A mid-November morning, grey and cold;

a drop of rain from the razor wire strikes a shoe, a

note to remember this day by, as Lowry people in

Laurel Hardy clothes, figures in ill-fitting blue go

in circles around a concrete centre in a slow

Auschwitz shuffle. On the perimeter, the ever-

watchful crows, always on the alert.

We walked in the Summer fields, you and

I, laughing in the tall grass,

the Sun was warm in the clear sky,

and we were happy.

In all the natural World,

we were happy creatures,

together in our time;

but we were young then,

and that was long ago,

for now, when I walk,

the fields are cold;

and when I look for you,

you are nowhere to be found.

8

In the midst of my numb feelings, I told our

Son, and my Husband's other children too, that their

Father had simply gone away on business, and

would be back as soon as he could, even though I

knew it could be years before they would see him

again. I did it that way because he and I both

wanted to protect them from the ignominy of his

disgrace, as well as the pain, though of course, they

felt the loss of him being there. Every Saturday, his children would come to be with me, as if things were entirely normal, and one good thing about that, was his children and I became close, and still are to this day.

It was hard acting as if nothing had changed, yet knowing what he must be going through every hour of every day he spent away from us all. I had no idea what his experiences were in those places where he was locked up like an animal, fighting for survival among the worst of us, but I was sure that one day he would return to us. What I didn't know – how could I? – was that he would never truly return to us in the way he left. The separation and separate experiences we had were to create a void that could never be filled, and hurts that could never truly heal.

9

Plunging now, into the dark pond of
Brixton, that unforgettable sight, the first meal,
that first black night. That room, those faces,
Belsen for Brixton, separated by a fragile vote, the
comparison closer than you could ever dream, the
gas-chamber a razor's edge away. In civilised
Britain, surely this cannot be, but the proof is in
the ugly disgusting pudding, and to taste it is to
see, but until the great majority, the silent
vigilantes chew their own seeds in the fruit, rough
justice will prevail, brute force rules, legalised
thugs who mistake the uniform they wear as a
symbol of their own power. Sitting in between the
striped walls of their shitty cell, Fritz and his
brothers care nothing for these rambling thoughts.

They are already lost children, hardly even aware

of the other world, beyond its care or control.

They accept their sentences as facts, not to be

liked, or hated, just to be served. When the clock

allows, the game begins again, handbags and

clothes, credit cards and drugs, the tools of their

trade, the facts of their lives, which they juggle in

a circus ring of days, accepting the groan of the

crowd when the parcel falls. They live in the

nether world, taking anything to escape from this

place to that. The goods they grab from human

artefacts are hardly stolen at all in their voracious

eyes, simply a ticket for the journey that they must

take. Dear friends, grey ghosts, they are drifting

still in those unholy unwritten halls of the truly

lost.

I have played.

I have played this game.

I have played this game of thinking.

I have played this game of thinking there is
a reason.

Why do I think/feel?

What is "Why do I think/feel?"?

What is "abcdefghijklmnopqrstuvwxyz"?

A dog scratches in the earth.

He is making sense to himself.

WANDSWORTH

1

Handcuffed and cowed, in the bus again,

reaching the gates, lines of ominous eyes, fierce

dogs who guard the door that no one wants to enter.

The pack gathers, snarling, all manner of men,

hawk eyes that mock weakness, pain must be felt,

not shown. In this assorted box, a pre-dominance of

black, an underground guerrilla war on the streets. Then, more weary blankets, stained with semen find their way up the winding stairs that lead from the ghastly central hub to C wing, where four new faces mix together with imperfect results, but with relative relief. Then, at ten, the lights go out to the sound of marching feet, and only the harsh glow from the yard outside illuminates the double bars.

In the morning, to enquire about open prison, that crumpled Nirvana, the allocation officer is the man to see. Several forms away, he suddenly arrives with hate in his eyes for indiscernible reasons.

"In your turn!" he spits, and stabs a bayonet finger in the chest, till powerless terror fills the heart.

Oh Guinevere, the week that followed the

nuclear war, that first visit took place. Behind the tears on your lovely face, I remember a walk by the lake; terrifying glimpse of Camelot days, so long ago, so long ago. Ten minutes and no more, to view this Paradise, and then a month to contemplate Le Morte D'Arthur, and all that might have been.

But to piss in a pot is not any worse for you, Lancelot, than for a soldier or miner, and the stink in the morning of fifteen hundred buckets pouring their way down the sink eventually mixes with the smell of the bacon and eggs, and is swallowed with the last dregs of the powdered war surplus tea, washed away down the drain; but the horror and the dread, the despair and the anguish, are wrapped around the soul, and can never be washed away.

2

My father died, and I was there to see it. His last words from the hospital bed were "Turn that fucking light off!" I've often puzzled over what he was seeing. I should have felt some pity for him, but in my heart I could feel nothing but anger at what he had taken from me.

My mother and I eventually made a kind of peace, and I visited her nearly every week. But those eyes of hers were still glinting cold when she looked at me, and I returned her gaze with equal disdain and lack of warmth. Then one day, she died too, and just as I had predicted years before, she asked me to give her a kiss just before the moment. I couldn't do it, and she gripped my hand hard, narrowed those Chinese eyes, and breathed her last.

But she would never leave me.

3

6.30am, and for some, the morning arrives

unexpectedly, with an eye at the door and a call to

court. Further charges must now be faced in

concurrent despair. The mind asks panic-stricken

questions that can not, will not be answered by silent sentries with blank unsmiling faces. Only a cheerless breakfast and chained cuffs, then a white van that glides ghostly through the Christmas streets and daily crowds, so happily unaware, oblivious to all this (curious, perhaps). These tears that fall from a young man's eyes and down a sad moustache are squeezed out of his brain like juice from an orange, to fall on sweating hands soaked through to the skin and bone. Occasionally, a strategic detour is taken, along shallow side streets to collide with smudged inkspot faces that pass with no comment to the utterly alone.

Pause. Southwark. Adrenaline flows, mouth goes dry, the gate goes up, as the chain unwinds as the doors unlock. The young man flinches and jerks out of his seat. One taken away (goodbye, good luck). Resume. Ironic journey, so close to home, where lovers lie, or sit at tea, the roads to this world just out of reach, arms that move on celluloid, lips just out of sync. from speech. Stop.

Snaresbrook. "Three here, one for the annexe!" "File them through!" (Another voice). Thoughts of the ark, going two by two. The cell resembles a bus stop shelter, but with no known destination. Two from the old days in Brixton, looking up the hill, ten years to face, now to be 'weighed off' again for the sake of closing the files. So slowly, the hands of the clock reach High Noon. Three are shot, the first a burglar, whose face gives a lie to his grin. Then, an old man enters, crying, two months to him for theft, but everyone wickedly laughs, and someone says

"Fuck me! I've done more time in the back seat of a panda car!" Then again, blue plastic plates, and the drab meal is a disappointment to appetites starved of stimulation (normal food is normally a perk of court). By now the gladiators about to die are straining at the leash and pacing the floor, faces white as winding sheets, and finally after seven hours, the authorities discover, purely by chance, that they have the wrong man, and that all pain was pretence, though no official pardon will be forthcoming, no word of explanation deemed appropriate.

And for all the long journey through the fading light of the streets, no one says a word, never to this day a word. Till finally, back in the cell, almost pleased to be there, the day is thoroughly analysed, and found wanting.

How to escape from this body of

strange substance

these walls that will not move?

There is nowhere to go. Cells that scream

for release,

constipation of the soul,

claustrophobia of the self.

This gold smear on the wall

a product of someone's sun

that shines, and somehow survives,

even in a dark place.

It crosses each corner

but before it can be caught,

it flies out of the window

and into the sky.

Is there a new round of illusion?

A box to play with,

while ruminating, thinking of games

won, and long ago lost.

4

Perhaps we just surround ourselves with

illusions, pretend that everything we have is solid,

when time so clearly shows that nothing is

forever. My life at home as a child, never happy,

and always tense, followed by my life in Preston Park, making me realise that things can always be worse. And indeed, worse was to come, returning home to find a monster there waiting for me, not just my father himself, but my mother too, and most of all, the feeling of living in that fear and the despair of not seeing what could be done about it. Each step was worse than before, so that when I met Michael, and we married and had a child, I can see now that we never stood a chance. I couldn't shake the feeling that had grown inside me, a monster of the Id, that was my own personal demon.

And my second husband too, he never really stood a chance, though this time we had love on our side, but I still had my demon, and now I had met someone who had his own, a whole den of them inside his head. The things that he had seen were a great help to me in understanding myself and my life, but it was a double-edged sword, pluses and minuses. He couldn't see these things without having gone there in his head, and if he had gone there in his head, how could he live a normal life? He couldn't, of course, and though our souls truly connected, we were doomed to failure. But it took a long time to get there, and while it lasted, the illusion was wonderful.

5

Ancient figures move silently on the

square, while a silver aeroplane glides across the

clear blue sky, through clouds too good to be true.

What would it be to live in that skyline once more,

as before with others? Now long gone, of course,

though sometimes, in the incontinence of

dreams……………

…………………..the slouching walkers with

pocketed hands pass the jackals who stand on the

corner, staring with hollow eyes, chattering,

waiting, watching with interest, as a casual trio

stroll, and calmly flick a bladed shaft across a

passing face that falls in tatters to the mud by the

side of the fence. All sound descends to silence,

the atmosphere eerie and tense. "He was a nonse"

it is said, in explanation; and as the officers on tip-

toes wait to collect the pieces, they are full of

trepidation. Two more circuits of the parade past

the place where a son of darkness lies.

6

She phoned me again, in the middle of
the night, and wearily we travelled to the dreaded
house, where every time I saw the stairs, I
remembered his footsteps, and there she was, half-
dead, but with those terrible eyes hardly bothering
to cover her wicked secrets.

We called the ambulance again, not
knowing till much later that this was indeed the last
time for such scenarios, the wolf had been called so
many times that the sheep merely waited to be
slaughtered.

When we had her installed in a bed, as ill

as she was, the first thing she wanted to do was smoke. So we struggled with her to the day room, and she lit a cigarette, making a big show of her final dramas, willing her hands to visibly shake, twitching her body as if she was in awful pain, a performance that increased in intensity the second a stranger was within eyeshot of her.

"Are you all right my dear?" asked the smiling uniformed ward sister, leaning over her patient, putting one caring hand on her shoulder. "Yes Sister, thank you", she said smiling an artificial smile which turned to a gash in her countenance as the Sister turned round and walked away. "Bastard!" she said, her face a contorted mask.

7

3am. In the half light, Jock is holding a

concert, standing on the table, and imaginary

microphone in his hand, and in between the lines

of the song, he clicks and rolls his tongue like sad

maracas (this is the sound of the backing track, he

explains). Thus he entertains his audience, a

disgruntled audience of three. As he reaches the

chorus, as if on cue, and aeroplane's lights

glowing red and green, can be clearly seen gliding

past the bars, the airliner's passengers blissfully unaware of the ants so far below. With a leap from the table, Jock runs to each bed, grinning ear to ear. Then nudging the arms of his sleepy companions, his smelly profile crosses the moonlight, parading in underpants with skid marks all down the back, and as with all his best performances, he rounds it off in the early hours by dropping a hefty shit in the corner, where no pot stands, leaving it to steam and settle till morning.

And the audience groans, and pulls the covers over their heads, pretending that they sleep, till finally they do.

8

It was strange to live alone after so many

years. The nights were the worst. In my fevered

imaginings, my father's footsteps would be heard

on the stairs, and I would see my mother's cold pig

eyes fixing me in their specimen gaze. How I

wished my companion was there! But he was down

among the dead men, and little did we know it at the

time, but it was the beginning of the end of us, for

part of him was never to return.

I hardly slept for a year, and used to pray

for morning to come. As soon as the light outside

showed itself, I rushed out of bed and opened the

curtains and drew the day into myself. The trouble

was, I knew that another night would soon be

arriving.

9

7.15am. The light goes on, disturbing

troubled sleep, and the situation reverses, for

being awake is the living nightmare to face with

each new day. Ten minutes later, the door unlocks,

unlocks again, and then swings open. Hundreds of

feet are already on the march along the landings

with buckets of slop; rows and rows of bleak

faces, queuing up to flush their buckets in a

battered off white sink. The cumulative effect of this stinking mass is almost physically in the air, and next to the sinks are the bowels being emptied, right there and then by the souls resigned to sitting it out on the seat with the hole in the middle, hardly protected from view. The flimsy doors barely cover the body, you can see the head and legs, so the masses lean over, and make droll conversation. "Nearly finished in there?"; "Got a Rizla, mate?"; "Any burn to spare?"

Then, rushing down the winding metal staircase with plates now streaked by permanent white, where the plastic has worn away with scrubbing; down, down, down, and down again, through the landing, four, three, two, one, running the gauntlet of officer's insults, to reach the mercifully covered tables, where a small cold greasy strip of bacon sits on a sad slice of concrete

bread. Then, all in reverse, till eventually, sucked

into the cells like air, the voices vanish.

10

What am I doing here with this man? He is

not either of my husbands, so who is he? I

sometimes wake and wonder at the strange turns

my life has taken. And why, when my beloved

cocker spaniel, Shane, died, was I more upset and

broken-hearted than I ever was for any man? Was

it because he gave me unconditional love, with no complications? And because he needed nothing in return but the feeling and warmth of my love, not the explicit physical expression of it? I mourn him to this day, yet that's life, isn't it? In bringing love to our lives, we invite death in for tea.

11

Late in the evening, during a game of

blackjack, every so often there is a loud 'smack' to

be heard. As the experienced explains to the

uninitiated, this is a 'shit parcel', a wrapping of

goods from somebody's arsehole, usually in

yesterday's news; a flying object sailing blithely

through the bars, calculated to land hard, to

splatter and scatter across the festering yard.

Over the roofs of these buildings, she lies,

A few miles,

But another time away.

12

Only three months had passed, but it felt like a lifetime already, with no sense of this nightmare ending. At nights, as the dark crept into the house, I would draw the curtains, switch on every light in the house, and turn up the volume on the television, hoping to blot out my thoughts and fears as much as anything else.

13

The view from the windows at

Wandsworth takes in the spattered huts, and down

below, the pathway to the showers, covered in

orange peels, stale bread, dead pigeons and shit

parcels. The sun can be seen, circling the sky, to

the soundtrack of the radio news, and the howls of the creatures in their cages. Down in the yard, a stream of traffic enters the showers, treading the pigeons, the bread, the endless shit into the mud and soggy tarmac that makes up the battered path. Seen from the outside, all these tiny faces are almost comically stuck high on a concrete wall. Forced on concentrate on small matters, senses heighten, as if on LSD, birds can be seen copulating in minute detail.

Beyond the huts is the small yard where rule 43, the nonses walk. White-faced, weird-looking creatures, made strange by their isolation, ironically playing the part, stereotypes, sentenced to food full of spittle, and tea, sweetened with glass. This is a legacy of perceived perversity, and they have the certain knowledge that somewhere in the dark, the cutter waits, and will not fail to leave his mark.

But much of the time there is no sound at all, just the ticking over of a brain on the red edge of explosion, eyes bulging, like an ant being eaten alive, old soldiers in a trench, sharing a hellish journey among the flying shells and bric-a-brac nonsense, the Jocks of this world, for example, raving in the corner, singing on the table, shitting on the floor, or broodily sulking on his bed, the silence as bad as the sound of his voice; oh Father, why have you forsaken us?

14

When he walked away from Preston Park

and left me there without a word, I had something

of a revelation. I was only ten, but in my inner

tears, I realised that my father was just a weak and

stupid man, not some God who ruled over our

lives.

Yet because he was my father, he had that

absurd power over me, and when he behaved as he did, I was helpless in his exercise of that power. His relative strength weakened me when I needed to be at my strongest. I was a frozen paralysed being with no movement but my own shaking, convulsed body, and no thought but terror, fear, despair, loathing, shame, outrage!

For years I wished I had the strength to kill myself, but the children cut off that possibility, and in any case, I was utterly determined that they should have the childhood I never had, the one that my friends all seemed to have taken for granted.

I used to envy them, with their quiet, patient, thoughtful fathers, and their doting mothers who fussed over them. Sometimes it made me quite angry that these friends of mine had never experienced the pain, loneliness, terror that I had. Yet I couldn't tell them anything, other than the hints that could be found in my often cynical remarks and sarcastic jibes whenever any deep happiness threatened to reach me.

My new husband was the first to crack something of that shell, and I even learned to relax at times, though the old fears still drove me, even with those two ghastly people called my parents in their graves. I slept rarely, and always had to leave the marital bed soon after we settled for the night, so much so, that my husband insisted I had another room set aside for my nocturnal roaming. My escape hatch, he called it, and he was right. That was one of the great gifts he gave me, one I treasure still. There were many others, but there were, as I said, two sides to this Faustian pact.

15

The smell of piss on a spring evening floats

gently across the floor. He shakes his dick in the

bucket one more time, and with a heavy sigh, he

flops on the bed. His red-rimmed eyes speak

eloquently of his desperation. He drinks his tea, and

eats a current bun, making a noise like an anteater

sucking a tree. Gentle Nigerian, he asks God for

forgiveness in loud whispers, and vows to repent, if

only granted parole. The, satisfied, he lays the book

aside and dreams of swindles and money to be

spent. So sensitive and proud, his name called

aloud, he lies and says that all is well.

Then he turns his head to restless sleep, as the

light switch clicks, and the dark comes on to the

sound of metronome feet, parading the corridor

outside.

A friend is someone

who shares the pain of confinement

during a dirty calendar,

and more than this,

makes plans for business expansion,

who painstakingly draws a whole scenario

and patiently rebuilds a sunset.

A friend is someone

who swears to make things right

when he leaves,

but when he leaves, he does nothing

but leave.

16

It felt so strange dealing with the neighbours, putting that face on, being 'normal'. But then, I had plenty of practice doing that for most of my life. Like most more-or-less abandoned or unwanted children, I had a hard edge inside me that almost nothing could touch. In some ways, looking back, I regretted ever getting close to him, the first person who had really touched me inside, but though he was closer to me than anyone had ever been before, he also understood that he could never truly reach me, I was too far gone for that. We all are, the children whose childhood has been taken away.

17

Brixton is blacker, but Wandsworth is an
ugly place, where the dogs are in human shape,
and the warders bite, bellow, and bark – CRASH!
The door swings open without warning, and the
unfortunate man behind is not quick enough to
move, like a hound in the wrong place, he is
kicked to the floor, and a wooden club goes
crashing against his ribs. Into the cell they come,
charging, barging, ransacking through the pathetic,
meagre goods, for who knows what. They seem to
find nothing, but instead, as compensation, they
drag the beaten man to the punishment block
where they will kick him black and blue to
complete the job, but time heals, and indeed, in
time, he will duly appear in court to answer

charges of assaulting those, who in reality, assaulted him. Such is the measure of justice meted out here, where absolute power is the order of the day, no prisoner's word carries any weight, the warders do as they please, and the governor knowingly condones, for good order is more important than justice can ever be. And now at the end of this drab day, the dark comes early to this corner of waiting.

18

The phone rang late at night, in the early

hours, in fact. "I'm dying" said the voice,

unmistakably Mother's. The next thing I knew, my

husband was calling out to me through a mist, and I

was covered in what seemed to be branches of a

tree. It was the Christmas tree, I had fallen into it. In

the background, there was a banging sound. It

turned out to be the dangling phone clattering back

and forward against the wall, its elastic loop acting
as a yo-yo, because I had dropped the receiver when
I fainted. It had been the noise of the phone and my
fall that had alerted my husband.

Slowly, I came round, more worried about
the pain in my head than the bruises from my fall.
With a slurred voiced, I explained what mother
had said, and, gathering our son, we rushed to
mother's house only to find her waiting calmly
with those chilling eyes fixed on us as if we were
thieves in the night.

"What did you come for?" she said, as
friendly as a rattlesnake about to strike. "Me? I'm
all right! I'm always all right!" she said,
indignantly, almost rising in her wheelchair, the
one she didn't't really need, it was only there for
effect and to garner sympathy when she needed it.

It was her substitute for no longer being sexually attractive, and she had that classic paranoid personality that believed her own lies, given enough time, and particularly when she had told enough people to make even the lies seem credible to herself.

That was the first of several false alarms, and she delighted in telling my brothers and sisters and Uncle Tom Cobbley that we had only hurried down there hoping to find her dead so we could rifle her house before anyone else got there.

She was a truly evil woman, and she was my mother. That thought alone pained me almost more than any other. Almost.

My poor dog, he suffered so at the end. Yet Mother and Father both went relatively quietly, it seemed so unfair!

19

A cold wind blows across the small yard as a helicopter circles above the crowd. Standing at strategic corners are the black-clothed watchers, staying by the sheltered places, irritable, rubbing hands, shuffling feet, disgruntled. Then, out of the blue, a man with a dark face turns and suddenly flashes a gleaming blade in a deadly precise arc into a white neck, and the red blood sprays the air as the figure falls heavily to the ground and is trampled by the crowd who cannot stop the stampede; and the watchers freeze, and turn pale, but remain inanimate. Till eventually, moving in slow motion, three of their number cautiously approach the stricken man, and almost like a funeral procession, like a dream, carry him beyond the doors and out of sight.

20

At times in my life, even now, I feel like I'm going mad. It's always been like that, and I seriously worried about my sanity many a time. How I survived that time alone, I'll never know. Yet in some ways, it did me good, as most bad experiences do. It teaches you something, makes you hardened, yet of course, it takes so much away from you too, things that you never get back. So many regrets.

21

The door bangs closed, the locks click, while the wind outside grows cold, and the day becomes dark. In this tiny space, seven steps down, three across, repeated over and over into a march of many miles. Then, the lights go out, and the animals howl. Some are laughing, some are crying, some are screaming, some are shouting out the window to their friends in their own peculiar language, a convict rhyming slang, an attempt to invent something that can be uniquely their own, a subconsciously desperate move to confirm their slender existence, and make themselves important to themselves.

Then, a bang outside, as a parcel goes past the window. It's time for night-time treats, as swinging ropes made from sheets make excruciating journeys along the wall to deliver shampoo, fruit, and stranger delights, while strategic brooms stick out of the windows to catch the prize that earlier, could have been hander over. All this to an orchestra of curses and yelps, a menagerie of noises from the throat and worse; John the Schnork next door, strongly schnorking, playing his catarrh at full volume among this melee; Jim the fart is breaking the wind noise record over land and sea; Steve the spit is gobbing the path at will; the sequence builds into a kind of cacophony that seems to threaten to take over the world; till, for those who no longer wish to hear these farcical sounds, a radio is placed against the ear, and slowly, another day disappears up the judge's arse.

22

At one point, I got so bad, they put me in Athlone house, in a strait jacket. No-one knowing me now or then would believe that. I seem so in control, and not a hair out of place, but I tell you, many a time I nearly lost my mind completely. It was all inside me, like the portrait of Dorian Grey in the attic. Outwardly, I was as perfect as could be, groomed to perfection, manners, deportment, bearing, all absolutely intact, but inside, I was a raging inferno! Or when I wasn't that, I would be an automaton, moving and existing, but not really alive, performing tasks as a machine would do, with wooden feelings to match.

My husband mainly left me alone, but not out of goodness. He was like that too, if he didn't find a space to curl up in, particularly a dark space, he would drink too much to compensate, and all the old invective would come out at full throttle. Not directed at me, you understand, but I was the audience, there was no escape from this unwanted performance. It made me feel even more insecure than I was, uneasy, almost as if I was drifting back to that house where the woman with the cold eyes lived, and where we all lived in dread of her nasty husband, but me more than the others, for his sinister footsteps only led to my bed, not my sisters nor my brothers. I was the one reserved for that special hell from which there is never any complete redemption.

And these ravings gave me some of the feelings of that past, and I instinctively recoiled, seeking my own space, not his, where I sometimes found him hiding in the cupboard, using darkness as a cover to pull over the head of his pain, that's why I sought my own things among everything we shared, something that was purely mine, my own, my garden, my beloved Shane – not his dog, our dog – mine.

And our child was mine too, his by name, yes, but he was an added extra, not the real parent, I was both parents to our Son, no-one else would ever get near him, he was never going to suffer the fate I had.

And being him, he realised all that without words being spoken, and in some ways it suited him, for he had an excuse to retreat and leave me to it, and he did, but not without resentment on his part. For he knew that he was third in the pecking order in my house, the children, the dog, then him, though he also knew I loved him as much as I ever

could love anyone.

I think we both understood the nature of

things, our particular problems, as they came to

be. For a time, life pulls in your direction, then it

withdraws its support, and you're on your own.

23

Sunday at Wandsworth. The strike is on,

the police are coming in. There is an unnatural

silence now, a tension so tangible it can almost be

physically touched, growing by the hour into a

solid beast. No sound of the least conversation nor

animal cries, as the light in the grey sky begins to

fade and darkness creeps over the high razor wire,

stealthily approaching the sombre building.

Then it begins. A faint rumble at first, like distant thunder, an ominous noise, like the hooves of a herd of unspeakable monsters, coming closer and closer, as it builds into a frightening, almost thrilling crescendo of fists and feet on fifteen hundred doors, a sound that dominates the air. Now, in parallel, the roar begins; more than a thousand voices, combining as one, like a demented football crowd. It comes out of the giant throat as one ghastly scream, making the blood curdle, the skin crawl, the scalp tingle, as the hair stands on end. For seemingly endless minutes, this runs at a full grisly climax, giving a feeling of the world about to spin from its axis and end. Then, as if by signal, a sudden brooding silence, almost as painfully tense as the bellowing of the beast. A heavy gloom now stalks the walls and corridors of this haunted house, almost as if the suppressed and restless subconscious minds had gained a monstrous combined life of their own in one unbelievable shape; murder is in the air, for any but the deaf and blind of spirit to feel and be aware of; time goes by in this cauldron of emotions, as if it were the fuse of a bomb, patiently sizzling, leading to an explosion of incredible force. The energy created feeds on itself, as the beast, having flexed its muscles, realises its own strength after so long in chains.

This terrible silence lasts a long time, and finally ends when policemen in full uniform are seen in the corridors by those who can look through the Judas hole. The rumbling begins again, a terrifying din, this time mixed in with the cries and howls of rage and hate, almost like a physical force battering against the vulnerable-looking policemen. Their faces are pale, they look terrified. If these doors were to give way, their lives would not be worth a penny, they would be torn limb from limb, and they know it, they feel out of depth in this alien environment.

During this first evening, the noise and the silence alternate, and each is as bad as the other, a cloud of depression and evil energy settles over the place, and almost as if it were the film of a book by Edgar Allen Poe, the black crows fly through the friendless beams of the yard lights like harbingers of doom.

Midnight comes, the cell lights go out late tonight, and one almighty noise swells through the building, fit to take the roof off, and then the sound simmers away petulantly, leaving pounding

hearts to settle till morning.

24

Days followed days, nights followed

nights. Nothing seemed to have any substance, no

form, no shape. I couldn't get my head round what

was happening, or where we would all end up. But,

as always with me, I had to keep up the damn

pretence to all around that everything was fine,

normal, no problem. If only they knew the way my

head was working!

25

C wing gratefully squeezes out into the yard,

exploding with relief, like corks out of a bottle. The

squads of police now file out behind them, and are

immediately showered by a virtual rainfall of

stones, which they nevertheless do their best to

ignore. Exercise then carries on, circle after circle,

till one man goes into a frenzy, attacking another, as

the policemen look on, aghast, unsure of what to do.

There is a surge en masse, as hordes of inmates

suddenly turn like a tide towards the few policemen,

who disappear under the howling mob.

Pandemonium breaks loose, the sirens go, the doors

and gates break open as scores, hundreds of

policemen charge through with truncheons drawn,

rushing towards the heaving mass of bodies, feet,

and fist, that breathes in and out like some terrible

living combined harvester gone mad; they go flying

in, hitting everything they see, forcing the melee

through the gates, back to the cells, fighting all the

way.

Down in D wing, the same thing is

happening, and blood flows freely, adding a gory

colour to the grey surroundings. Finally, after a vicious battle, order is restored, and the doors are banged shut. By the time the police commissioner arrives to walk among the debris like Christopher Plummer as the Duke of Wellington in the film 'Waterloo', an eerie calm hangs like a mist over the grey battlefields of Wandsworth.

26

In horror, I read the news about the strikes in Wandsworth

– That's where my husband was! As if things weren't bad enough!

But one thing I knew about him was he was tough in those ways at

least. He would survive. What I didn't know and what scared me –

with good reason as it turned out – was what it was doing to him

inside his head, his heart, his soul. We would all pay a price for

that, but him most of all.

27

The strike now enters its final phase;

weeks of total confinement are coming to a close.

Life becomes solid, 'normal', the place calms

down, no more noise from the blank grey walls,

no more animal cries through the lonely bars; but

still in force, the gruelling regime, 24 hours,

trapped there, like a dog with a dirty coat, and still

no place to rest a weary arse, so tired of tissues in

waste paper baskets, and the aroma of buckets

now covered in stains floats across the room like a

friend whose company is wearing thin.

It is Sunday; the procession passes through

landing one, and round the grid lined with solemn

warders. The return to order has been slow, the

regime cautious. Now the familiar barks echo in

the tall structures of the glass dome, but still there is a hushed insolence as C wing strolls into the open air of the yard, breaking into shuffling groups of dark shapes. The day outside is cold, dull, downcast, and the warders shiver in their shoes, as well they might; only ten minutes of circles, then to their right, an argument begins. The second officer intervenes, a classic mistake, he calls the loudest over to his side, and with a pointing finger, he lays down the law. Immediately, a hush surrounds the crowded yard, the atmosphere so deep, so tense, a cutting edge. Then, the man is sternly warned, and sent back, scowling to the fold. It seems as though the incident may now pass, but suddenly, two in the centre of the circle are squaring up to one another, a glass bottle miraculously appears in a hand, it smashes against a post, but will not break, then thumps several times against the ground, to get no response but laughter from the grim spectators, gathered all around. Then comedy becomes tragic, the glass gives in, and the myriad edges marry to a face, as blood and screams convert the silence into pandemonium. All hell breaks loose, the warders rush as one, and as they rush, are rushed themselves, sucked in like a vacuum by the deadly hordes; whole packs are diving, snarling, on black-clothed bodies, tearing, ripping, kicking, punching, gouging; blades appear, and begin to flash across the yawning flesh that lies writhing, helplessly beneath, creating wounds that will never heal. Now help arrives to answer the urgent screaming of the sirens, a virtual stream of prison officers begin the charge of the light brigade to rescue fallen comrades from further damage; the truncheons fall on any head to hand, for the innocent as well as the guilty must share the blame. The mob begins to fragment, and gradually disintegrates, only the truly lost persevere – there in the middle, a man with yellow hair battles increasingly alone, like Custer's last stand, till finally, he succumbs to superior numbers, and disappears in a hail of raining blows. Already, a slow trail begins to straggle through the doors, the war outside is coming to a close, each man is searched and roughly pushed back through, the heroes and villains, assembled in their roles.

It is Sunday; and after tonight, when the curtain falls on today, will tomorrow's eyes still recognise the face the mirror sees?

ARUNDEL

1

Into a dark gateway, a few lights among

the blackness of a stormy night, out into the

blasting rain, across an incomprehensible road,

and into a large dirty dining area, where crude

food awaits. Then, herded inside and empty pre-

fabricated unit, where a solitary TV set stands,

high on a shelf, looking tiny and lost among the

scattered metal chairs and dusty concrete surfaces.

Through the vacant staring window frames, a full

moon gazes, giving an eerie effect, heightened by the ghostly bluish glow of the flickering screen, the thin treble sound resonates into the high ceiling, the music and voices compressed, nasal, remote, sound waves from Saturn. The overall effect is of the aftermath of the apocalypse, in a bomb shelter housing the last television on earth. The unsettling atmosphere spoils any pleasure at seeing this relic from days of happiness.

And as they wander in lost hordes around the perimeter road, where the wind howls and moans, like a lonely spirit flying over the high fence to sweep across the deserted cricket field, the scarecrows in ill-fitting denim who drift through the dark in aimless circles, still face desolation in this desert of a place.

2

I heard much later, in one of his letters, about his move to the South Coast, further away from me than ever. But at least, he reasoned (trying to reassure me, as always!), he would have more freedom, not be locked up so much, be able to walk around, and not be locked in. That wasn't quite true, of course. Though his immediate door wasn't locked, the building door was, and there was still no escape from the dreadful people, the ones who the only remedy for is to be locked up like that, the ones who are natural predators, unfeeling animals who prey on anyone they can, without a thought for anyone but themselves. "Arseholes" was the word my husband used for them. By that, he meant people who cared not a jot about anyone but themselves, including family, children, human beings, animals, anything was expendable to their needs.

3

The bell rings three times, and it's an early

rise, struggling out of coarse green blankets to a

morning of lashing rain, wearing a donkey jacket

with blue shoulders. After the endless bells and

parade, an amazing walk across a real road, where

normal people drive their cars. One longing look

along that stretching road to the horizon, then on

to the estate path to another day in the salt mines,

infinite days lining along the future, the weary

clock striking the hours of yet another week, as the

early morning train passes in the distance, and a

silver aeroplane plays tricks in the sky, looping the

loop, and swooping up and down in astonishing

gestures of freedom. Here, down to earth, the day

goes on, the same as the day before, and the day

before that; even when old Dave has a stroke, a

harness is put on his useless hand, and he still

must shuffle his dragging leg through all the same

procedures – no concessions; illness is not an

excuse, just a nuisance; dying is not permitted till

the earliest day of release.

So, the bells, the parade, to repeat the

entire performance; the road, the path, the road,

the queues, the bells, the parade, the perimeter

road, the darkness, the days over and over and

over and over and no one in this strangulated

hernia of a home has ever been so alone.

4

I visited him. It was horrible. I thought he

was going to break down, he looked ghastly, his

eyes, always filled with dark mysteries, were now

gateways to hell, and his face was gaunt and

strained, he had suddenly lost a great deal of

weight. Harry was with me, but the poor man hardly

knew what to say or do, words between my husband

and I were agonising noises that somehow were squeezed and wrenched from us. Being as close as we were to each other, the instinctive knowledge of what was inside each other's heads kicked in, and almost overwhelmed us. He told me years afterwards that he was fine, he was surviving. What he had found most difficult was seeing the person he loved there, in that pit and pendulum of a place. The two didn't go together, he said, light and dark co-existing. But then, he always did put me on a pedestal.

5

A deserted place, an oasis away from the maddening crowd. Del and Glyn meet here in silence, drawing strength from each other and the Fellowship room. Glyn is a builder trapped in a snare, living for the day beyond the gate, his proud heart crushed and metaphorically leaning against the fence. Del, on the other hand, sees fate as something he has brought on himself. Quiet, yet strong, he carries Glyn along, cheering the soul with poems and songs and hopes for a future that he, in reality, does not have.

6

Apparently he made some friends in there, or so he said. For a man who was so tough in ways, so resourceful, so insightful, he could be incredibly naïve, was my thought about it all. He always chided me when I accused him of that, saying no-one could be more cynical or aware of human behaviour, but if you didn't open the door to the possibility of other actual human beings who weren't 'arseholes', then you were losing something of your own soul. Something, I'm afraid, that could be well ascribed to me.

7

The little yellow man is a good worker;

polite and well thought of as convicts go; but none

of this prevents his sudden seizure at an

unexpected hour and his rapid internment in the

block. He is to be deported to Thailand, and his

tears and his terror are terrible to behold. His

claims of torture and death when he returns are

met with blank stares and silence, and regardless,

next day he is dragged forcibly to reception,

screaming his head off, trembling in panic and

fear, fighting as if for air, while the unwilling

onlookers shudder at this ghastly sight. Till at last,

his voice and trauma are swallowed by the

insistent waiting taxi, as he leaves under heavy

escort to whatever fate awaits him.

8

It was late summertime, almost autumn,

and he had been gone so long now, it seemed so

long.....but now, I was going to meet him, steal a

short interlude from the authorities, be with him in

every way possible. I waited in the car, and saw him

walk up the long lonely road from Rustington and

his community service, heading back towards that

desolate craphole, and even though he wore shabby

clothes and looked pale and drawn, the sun shone

on us that day for those pathetic few minutes we spent in the back of the car. As the leaves swirled around the windows, we made love, almost in consummation and affirmation.......when I think back to that now, our clinging to each other during that bright interlude, it makes me sad to think of how futile, how puny our efforts are in holding back the tide...........

The man on parade is looking strange; he

is sweating, and though black, he is almost turning

white. He struggles for composure that he does not

have, sways and rocks, like a puppet with faulty

strings, and eventually, he collapses in a broken

heap. He is carted off by unsympathetic hands,

who know only too well what has gone wrong; he

has newly returned from home leave, and has

deliberately swallowed a wrapped up parcel of

drugs, that he intended to collect from the outflow

of his bowels, scraping among his very shit for

gold. Unfortunately for him, the wrapping has

come undone before its passing, and a massive

overdose nearly kills him off. He will recover, but

waiting when he does are further years upon years,

with parole not on the agenda, and back to

Wandsworth, with no prospect of relief, other than

being alive, or this version of life at least, like

being in an iron lung, breathing, but not much

else.

And this is a common method of bringing

in contraband; the ten pound notes that circulate

freely are mostly stained with shit; they are

swallowed on a visit, and then must be scraped

from the doings every day, when the vending

machine finally reveals the jackpot, which is not-

too successfully cleaned, but will suffice to buy

the goods that otherwise would not be there. For

vodka is delivered at the back of the fence, and a

'postman' is paid to collect by being out of his

billet beyond the hours of curfew. A game then

ensues of cat and mouse, for the officers know

what these moves are, the patrols by the fence are

irregularly timed to catch the postman out; and

many a parcel is seized, and many a postman

posted, but drink flows freely just the same, and

the shitty notes pass from arse to pocket in this

grisly game of barter.

10

At times like this, you find out who your

real friends are. Anyone who has had a drastic life

experience will tell you that, and it's true. People I

thought I could depend on vanished like flies, and

the opposite is also true – Some people you

considered as lesser friends were the very ones who

were there for you, no matter what. I learned an

awful lot in those years about friendship and

betrayal. It's a true thing to say that it's only in grief

and pain you move forward in your mind, your

spirit, your knowledge of what life really is, or

should be. I've never been religious or Godly –

Something my husband always berated me about –

But I do believe him when he says that God exists

and that we are here for a purpose. It's just so hard

to live up to his expectations, or even your own.

11

The lifer gets into an argument over queue for the phones. He is tall and spidery, with black empty eyes like pissholes in the snow, an arrogant type who thinks that his special status gives him clout. The argument is heating up, going out of control.

"Do you know what I'm in here for?" demands the lifer, in a haughty, threatening tone.

"Yes" replies the other man, "Because you're an asshole".

12

My father was a sewage worker. Now, my
sardonic self sees that as appropriate, a metaphor
for who he really was. But my husband pointed
out to me that bad as he was in his behaviour, he
was something of an innocent party in what
happened. He was just weak and stupid, and to

some extent, he himself didn't understand the forces that drove him to behave as he did towards his own daughter. If that's what I was.......for I know my mother was a plaything of the town doctor, and many people have remarked on what a cuckoo I look, nothing like my sisters or brothers, so it makes you wonder.......

I'd certainly like to think I was nothing to do with this ghastly man who was labelled 'father'. I saw that film 'Spit on his grave' and I'd subscribe to that, but then, I'm not as understanding as my husband about these things. He said that his theory was my father actually loved me, but when he expressed it, my mother's jealousy was fearsome to behold, so being who he was, to please her, he was hard on me, showed me no love, as was her way........in his later years, when he became impotent, his sexual frustrations and fears then expressed themselves horribly on me.........I listened to all this, and though I believed my husband – he was talented in these insights – it didn't bring me any closer to a vision of peace in the proceedings, or to any measure coming anywhere near closure. As I said, I'm not as understanding or forgiving about these things as my husband is. But then, it didn't happen to him. It happened to me.

13

Now the storms of Spring have ended; the

sky is brightening, the sun begins to come

through, warming the bleak white huts that sit so

artificially on the grass. Donkey jackets disappear,

and bodies begin to brown, everyone clamours for work on the estates, and still the swift turnaround goes on, regiments of people appearing, disappearing, and among them, one neutral morning, Del says his final goodbyes, that mythic day unbelievably here at last. His logical mind no longer able to operate, he stands at the crossroads with watery legs, and says goodbye to Glyn, and then, along that path he goes, growing smaller and smaller, his pack upon his back like a fairy-tale gnome, he goes, turning and waving every few yards, already feeling survivor's guilt, until the corner of the reception building swallows him up, and he vanishes forever from this land.

Dear Friend, Brother, fellow traveller,

The caravan is here,

You must leave now,

It's clear and logical, as you know, to leave

This place of dead dreams,

Where, nevertheless, beautiful ideas can

still grow.

Go into the brightness, begin your journey,

It's a day you should be born,

You must leave now,

This morning arrives on time, no bells can

ever

Stop the sun from turning

Its shining light to warm and grow in the

coldest cells.

Bells and celebrations! We, your

companions

Mark this summer day,

You must leave now,

There may be still so much unspoken, and
yet

Though part of you must go,

A part of you remains, the circle is closed,

the links unbroken.

A token of friendship, this poem, our

Brother,

Also to be free,

You must leave now,

And we, though sad, will bless the

dawning of this

Day, and wish you joy,

Wondrous sights await you on the shores

of such a morning!

14

When things settled down for us, when the
money came along, and we could seemingly live the
kind of life we had dreamt of, felt entitled to, for
that time, it was Camelot. I spent my days planning
work on the house, plotting my garden, buying fine
clothes. The strange thing is that the closeness
between us wasn't as it had been in the struggling

years. Our independent spirits were now haughty enough to feel that we were indeed people of the world, who need have no fear nor favour in dealing with anyone else – not even each other.

He was, as usual, lost in his plots and plans, and with the success being so spectacular thus far, he had every right to lock himself away from me and our son, and indulge himself in fancy thoughts and schemes. I was defeated in that respect, but my compensation was the keys to the candy store. Even then, something in me told me it was wrong, something wasn't right. I begged him time and time again to save money, to hold back for the future, my insecurities were screaming at me 'Where's the catch?'!!!! But he just placated me with fine words and confident posturing. He was good at that sort thing, and in fairness, I think he believed it himself. But, just for a change, I was

right this time.

15

If Wandsworth is hell's engine room, then

Ford is the waiting room of despair – take a look

at the props:- the visitor's reception area, so clean,

and almost pleasant, the public face of another

ghastly façade. The visitors immediately feel that

life here can't be all that bad; but behind the

glittering teeth of this place are a set of rotted gums; figures like tramps trudge along the littered paths and wearily past the worn-out wooden huts that squat above the empty whiskey bottles like an ugly aunt, caught with her pants down, while inside the dirty corridors and cracked walls, the defeated rooms and half-dead sinks stand silently waiting for the return of the hopeless crowds from their conveyor belt of drudgery, creeping along through their small segment of time, as the wheels turn, the wheels turn, the wheels turn. The rusted machinery, the grinding pneumatic limbs still somehow functioning for this mechanical day, exactly like so many others.

To wake yet another switched-on morning, plunging downstairs to be among the first in the queue; standing like lamp posts at the dining hall entrance, watching dumbly, with half-awake feelings as the allotted workers with the wide brooms systematically sweep the morning's collection of dead cockroaches that lie with their legs in the air across the tired floor that curls at the edges like a British Rail sandwich. The silence is only broken by the swish of the brooms, and the crunch of heavy boots, squashing some of the huge insects on the floor in the effort to shovel the majority into the galvanised buckets, and out to the furry dustbins in the scrap heap of a yard.

The bell rings once, the signal to run, the scramble for the eggs and bacon has begun. The jousting begins, the brazen take a walk to the head of the queue, gambling on bare-faced cheek and fear of lost remission. Then come the con-men, reading a nearby notice board, then slipping into the queue, fooling no one but themselves. Now and again, and officer pulls a man out, sending him to the end of the line, out of personal animosity, rather than discipline. For discipline is inconsistent, and of no consequence to the general melee. Animal behaviour in all its forms is here, and on display, even those who consider themselves well-bred are not innocent of naked greed. There is no honour among thieves; they would strip one another of everything, given the chance. They cajole and hector those of their kind who are called on to serve, demanding more than they could ever need or want, knowing that punishment for the kitchen man's compliance is banishment, or worse. They feel no remorse when this happens, as long as they have more than their share; they feel content, if only for one greedy moment.

In truth, they are rats fighting over a rotted carcass; the porridge is made from pig's meal, the bacon is a lump of grease, swimming in its own body fluids, and the egg is a despairing plop from a constipated hen. This then, is the prize the mob will kill for, cooked with cockroaches and all, something to focus on, perhaps, for nothing much else happens here, work, eat, sleep, in endless rotation, decorated by a drone of conversation and gossip, a constant stream of verbal excrement, dribbling on and on, punctuated by occasional incidents, like fights about the phone, or people 'blocked', 'shipped', 'nicked'. Circles and circles of perimeter walks, ghostly visits to TV rooms, everyone desperate to find a corner of something that isn't there; the ludicrously civilised cricket matches on the same summer field, and the visitor's teams, come to the zoo to see how the other half lives. Polite applause incongruously mixed with a spit or worse from an untutored spectator who sees no reason for niceties in this stunned dressed-up broken brain of a place. For they still lock the gates of the field when the visitors look the other way, and after the cricket, tea, and scones, the home side are hunted into their pens, their PR use suspended, they become once again, the animals they are, till the cupboard and gloves must be used, yet one more weary time.

16

Mother. I could write books about mother by myself. She was born of an English mother called Alice, who had a sad and terrible life, thanks to her husband, an Italian immigrant, who got drunk and beat her and abused her in full sight of the children. Alice died very young, of cancer. At least she was then free of that monster who called himself her husband. So I suppose you could say that my mother was traumatised by the events of her childhood – for all I know, she too was abused by her father in more ways than just physical, perhaps it was sexual too. But I can't feel anything that lets me forgive her. After all, you could explain the forces that drove Hitler to do what he did, but it doesn't excuse it. Some of us – many of us – carry

terrible secrets, but we don't take it out on others,
and certainly not on our most beloved children.
Sometimes though, we take it out on our partners in
life……..

My husband always said that my mother
had two faces, the one she showed, and the other in
the attic, the one with the twisted mouth and terrible
countenance. Occasionally, the face of the monster
would show itself, not just in appearance, but by
words and deeds. Near her end, she claimed that
newspapers were carrying photographs of her
saying what a wicked women she was. Perhaps the
truth was squeezing through into that awful heart.

I'm glad she's dead, but the trouble is, she
still walks in my mind. Even when I look in the
mirror, I can see her eyes staring at me……..

17

A letter from Del, so strange to receive.

He's now one of 'them', a fabled creature from the

outside world, and Glyn feels the strain even

more, a bad day in a bad month of a bad year, a

sentence for tax, at the time of his father's death,

he is like an eagle that cannot fly, his spirit being

drained by an enemy he cannot fight with his fists.

The letter from his friend makes him sad and

happy all at once; six weeks, and he too will be

free, but this is no comfort to his restless soul.

Even seeing the plight of others too scared to hope

cannot raise his heart; but even the authorities

cannot stop the clock, and clicking whirring

clanking machinery of the skies duly turns the

weary gears, until one knock-kneed morning, Glyn

finally goes home.

Waiting like an animal

to be released; fearing

the unseen enemy

he cannot fight; becoming

duller by the day;

in that dark corner

of his haunted mind, there,

in a room with cold bare walls

and ceiling cracked with age,

as the moonlight shines

through the window

curtains never graced, he sits

on the edge of an unmade bed,

his hands on his head, gripped

by the talons of despair.

Believe it

or not, nothing can stop

the eagle from flying

Again.

18

My husband was so confident in his new friends; I suppose that came from his inner belief that everything had a purpose, there was a fate to it. So he supposed that meeting Del and Glyn would be the most positive thing that could emerge from such a dark place.

But we had already experienced disappointment with another so-called friend, who promised so much, and did nothing at all, so I was not optimistic.

Del did call, but I could tell he felt under obligation, and was doing so reluctantly. I sensed that now he himself had fled that awful land, he was in no hurry to relive the experience through continued connection with those that he knew there.

I dared not say a word to my husband in my letters – I rarely went and visited him, he begged me not to, saying it was much too far away, and too much of a strain for both of us. I was just so sorry and sure that my husband was being idealistic, perhaps understandably clutching at straws, trying to find a reason why we were enduring such awfulness. Was it all for nothing?

19

It looks like rain, the sky is dark and

overcast, the clouds have a weary look about them

as they drift above the parade. The last bell has

gone, only the stragglers still join the crowd.

These are the days of parole, to be or not to be,

through the long wicked months of waiting, as the

summer wears on.

20

As we rolled into Winter, it was beginning to

seem that this was how life would be now forever.

There was no word of him coming home, as we had

hoped he would after one long year, which had

seemed a lifetime. How could some men spend twenty or thirty years and remain sane? I often felt like I was going mad sharing the experience, yet I, like everyone else on the physical outside of such an experience had no idea at all of what it felt like to be so imprisoned, so lost to humanity, to life.

My husband tried to explain to me afterwards that those of us who have bad days now and again, or even a bad few days, can't envisage a life where every day is like that, every day is a horrible black day filled only with survival and depression. I heard the words, but of course, until you experience it yourself, words are only words, not the real thing at all. Yet my husband's experience was but a mere fraction of what some have to endure – How can any human being be expected to be 'normal' on entering the world again?

21

'Tis Brillig, and the slithy toves are

wearing donkey jackets again; the weather

beginning to change now, the games are winding

down. Solitary figures walk in the rain endlessly

round the perimeter road. Weeks now, waiting for

release, avoiding like the plague those jubilant

figurers who have parole in their pockets. Some
are looking like shadows of themselves, gaunt and
cheerless, over their date, the pleas of their
families falling like leaves on the stone walls of
the Home Office, and meantime, the days and
weeks are slipping by, and no sign of it is
showing.

Then, darkness, and the bells on the
building ring and bring these figures to heel for
another curfew; the rain batters the windows as the
distant voices echo and fade among the corridors.

When the last gypsy wakes

from his slumber of gold,

from dreams like memories,

wrinkled and old,

dressed in the takes his Grandfather told,

the last gypsy wakes alone.

When the last gypsy talks

to the darkening sky,

to the Moon's reflection

in the river nearby,

when he sings to himself,

do you wonder why,

his eyes have turned to stone.

The last gypsy wakes alone.

22

Sometimes even now, as I lie in this new house with a new husband, I think of Vicarage, and our life there. It has all become unreal, yet it haunts me still – did I run away too easily? Did I take the time to truly examine my feelings, or did I just instinctively run just like I did from those heart-beating footsteps on the stairs?

When I think of him now, when I see him, he is living that ghost-life he always was on the verge of, the one he couldn't quite manage to when I was there. Perhaps I have set him free, to be a lost vagabond, a spirit who doesn't belong in this world.

I know I should move on and forget all this, and so should he. But neither of us can somehow forget that time or each other. Yet we have to live in a real world, a practical world, not one built on dreams, and not a house of cards. Our dreams of each other are/were spiritual dreams, not the substance of reality at all. And yet without that dream, without that sharing of souls, where is the reality?

23

A day at work disintegrates; the boy who

won parole the week before is about to have the

smile wiped from his face. He trades tobacco, as

many a man has done for barter before, but the

civilian in charge does not like Pakistanis, and

jumps on the chance to punish the scraggy youth.

The civvy's childish face contorts with indignant

rage, where, a moment before, he laughed and

joked with others who bartered in front of his

eyes. He grabs the offending item, and rushes to

make a charge, leaving the lad with a face as white

as an officer's shirt.

You find me wandering through my days

A ghost in the half-light

Struggling to see what is written down

Before the darkness brings the night.

24

Around this time, I think both of us began to truly despair. Perhaps it's all a phase we go through in any kind of grief – first, the unbelieving, the numbness; second, the shock, the horror; third, a horrible kind of acceptance of sadness so deep it can hardly be articulated for fear of complete breakdown; then, following all that, as the days and nights refuse to change, a kind of lost desperation and breaking down of the will, you begin to pray out loud for this torment to end.

Then perhaps, once those waters break, the process just begins all over again.

25

Trying to make sense of this; caught like a dog living with a violent master. Time now to take what little movement there is on this rocky shore, time to let this creature feed on someone else in the dark wild forest. Just as the weather is about to change, time to reach for those microscopic heights, community service.

To walk then, to the gate, to be summarily searched, then sent on the unthinkable way, beyond into the awesome unknown, without a cold hand on the shoulder, or a handcuff to be seen; this thrill, the open fields, swaying in the cool breeze, the station ahead in the distance; and still, the dread, the fear, the apprehension, waiting on the platform for a train, stepping aboard with someone else's feet; sitting, talking, living someone else's life, a stranger wearing the clothes.

Off, across the crossing, feeling conspicuous,

dressed like a tramp, aware of everyone's eyes.

Standing out in the high street, being frowned on

and ignored, like a man from Mars. Then, into the

home, where the victims of multiple sclerosis

await; a meeting of cripples and lepers, supervised

by the vigilant staff. The cook keeps a wary eye

on the convicts who shuffle their feet across her

kitchen floor like cockroaches. She throws out

orders as numerous as the tit-bits she feeds the cat.

"Who wants the prisoners?" she asks the

staff. The new Negroes have arrived. Scrubbing

like serfs to be accepted, a dozen mistresses to

serve, for who would be a slave to the slaves?

Then, a trudge to the station across wild

fields; walking briskly in the crisp air, leaving the

cook blissfully unaware of the easy path that leads

to such a fate.

26

Another letter arrives. He has met someone
at the care home, someone who thinks he has
talent, he is full of all that, but all it does is bring
me to despair. What good did all his dreaming do?
Why could I not find a man who could just do his
job and look after us all without having to feel he
had to rule the world, be feted, admired by his
peers? Do we have to be on television or in the
papers to prove we are alive and worthwhile as
human beings?

There was something missing in my
husband that way. He seemed to need the approval
of the crowd, the applause, the rewards, the
praises. In that way, we were opposites. I didn't
like ego, I felt I didn't have one myself. But as my

husband pointed out, if that was true, then why did

I care about what people thought of my clothes,

my hair, my skin, my very appearance?

27

The writer in the attic is here, for only a

short few weeks

He will guide the hand of a marvellous girl, trapped

in her body; and now, without prejudice, he offers

his hand to another prisoner. He remembers only

too well his days in the Japanese camps, and how it

feels to be truly alone.

He has seen such Sunsets, walked such

shores, fought battles in mind and skies; yet still

he sees the World and its creatures through fresh

and innocent eyes, always prepared to believe the

best, while remaining aware of the worst that lies

within us all. He take these hieroglyphics from a

native hand, and translates, as only he can, the

disjointed pictures scratched roughly upon the

wall.

Most of all, he brings hope where there was none, warmth where there was coldness; glowing words where there were only lonely sounds to fill the silence.

28

Somehow the cold nights coming
increased my loneliness. I rarely slept, just tossed
and turned, or got up and walked around in the
dark through all the rooms except my Son's. It
was as if I was looking for something in the house
that didn't exist anymore. It was as if I was only a

part-person, not whole at all.

Even when my husband and I finally separated, that other terrible time in the future, I had to have someone else there to share my days and especially my nights with. It didn't matter a jot that I didn't love this man – In fact, that made it better. All that mattered was he could work nine to five and provide a fine house and a comfortable living. All that could be achieved without my heart or soul being even scratched an inch.

29

Dark nights drawing in; Y hut, in the last

of these snapshot days; beneath the sign of the cat,

the 'next out' board that all must ritually sign. And

there, on the board, are the signatures of Del and

Glyn, so long gone now, it seems. A mock-reading

of 'The Minge Plant' follows, that poem

constructed by Del to amuse the fellows of the hut,

who loved him dearly; but he had a serious side,

one he could rarely show, and the deepest secret of

all stays hidden within his heart.

TO SIMON

I, who presume so much,

at a distance so far removed,

nevertheless must speak,

and bless them both,

to my friends, who beg silence,

in sincere peace, I send this prayer,

and call this torment of the soul to cease.

Forgive me this intrusion,

dear friends, whose pain I cannot

begin to understand;

how could I

possibly begin to imagine

how to cope, when the fact is –

He closed his eyes, and those eyes will

never open.

These restless seasons, the mind

struggling with changes the heart

cannot face, familiar

landscape gone

forever; such despair –

Where do we start? So much to remember,

these unrelenting days, twisting the heart.

The chimes ring out across

the water, and the echo

sails away –

Has time ended because we only hear

the silence? Doubt grows and grows,

hands that grip the soul, wringing it out.

Such devastation;

and yet, the world still spins,

the earth grows, continues,

keeps evolving,

though many of the changes

are out of sight; with cells I would not

know, a journey ago, this hand will write.

So difficult to express honestly,

Dear friends; the cycles cannot

be overturned by lack

of understanding;

the lines of communication

may be faint, but his joy must fly,

and his spirit must be free of such restraint.

Then, just before the bell, it's time to leave the hut, and go back into the darkness; back to the other buildings. Now, with the wind and the rain, and night all around, and Y hut receding in the distance, the men going their own separate ways, Del and Glyn and the summer seem like a story from another time.

30

And finally, that unbelievable news arrived. He was coming home. Though in some ways, it was a worse time, for no date was set, he was just told he had achieved parole on a date to be set soon. How cruel the Home Office is! They have all lived such a sheltered cossetted life that they have no idea of the pain and suffering their petty bureaucracy causes randomly every minute of every day to those poor unfortunate souls who have suffered so much.

Yes indeed, those who commit crimes must be punished, and especially those who do irreparable harm without thought or care to others, but the system is all-encompassing, and punishes everyone the same way, from petty misdemeanours to major murdering raping bastards – all are equal in the system's eyes, and indeed, the public see it that way too. Once tarred and feathered, there is no forgiveness or understanding, only hate and prejudice forevermore.

But where we were at that time, we did not yet know any of that. All we cared was that one day soon he would be home and life would resume. Only it wouldn't.

31

Inside Saint Bridget's, inside the bodies,

the true prisoners wait, each with a story to tell.

The lady model who wears incontipants, and sucks

her dinner through a straw; the man who was on a

plane, and found he couldn't get off; and so on,

and so on.

Now, through the clear silent hallways of

this plastic place, in their eerie wheelchairs, they

grimly pursue the human figures they perceive

will feed them, dress them, wipe their arse, or talk,

or light cigarettes – anything – in a muted version

of the old forgotten days when they were real, like

anyone else. The boy who drinks his tea from a

plate; the army officer who bites her clothes, for

trapped inside, is a human being, struggling to be

understood. The Scotsman with the hat, who came into the dining room that silent afternoon, just staring in silence, the day before he died, as if he somehow knew he was about to be released.

The days of Fellowship

are so long gone now; Y hut

and all that, consigned to dust. The sun

beats down on St. Margaret's church,

burning

the face, the skin turning red, the body that

sits, feet

at the foot of this place that hides him

from all eyes; all of this that is forever

him, existing now, in words alone. Those
steps

to freedom, so cruelly won, led finally

along the gravel path, to stop

by the side of the church.

A gentle breeze

rolls up the green slopes of Downham hill,

and rustles

the thinning hair; while the dead lilacs stir,

as if

for an instant, come to life, but nothing

else moves; and

this is how it will be now, the summer will

run

its course; autumn and winter will follow;

then

Spring; and another cycle will begin; year

after year, flowers will find their way here,

growing,

dying, being replaced, till even the last

flowers

wither, while the words fade on the stone,

and no one

who is anyone remembers; century will

follow century, yet

still, nothing will move, nor stir, but the

wind

and the weather, the rain, snow, and sun,

and those

who still breathe under the same sky; just

another

sweltering summer day, and all of this

that is forever lost.

HILLFIELD

1

These days, I live far from here, with yet

another new husband who lives in total ignorance

of the lives of these other women who were me, and all the better for it. He needs looking after, this one, it keeps me on my toes to be the one depended on, the grass is always greener, I suppose. I have my new house, and my new garden, and new things to do. But the same old things still bother me, and I miss him and worry about him.

When he came home, he was never the same. He was rude to the neighbours, embarrassing me, and picking arguments with people over next to nothing at all. That experience inside was the worst thing that could have happened to someone like him, he was bad enough as he was. Though we were still very close, and shared that place only he and I inhabit, there was now a wall between us that could not be broken down. The wall wasn't for me or for anyone else, it was around him alone, and there was no reaching him.

Things ran their course, and I had to say good bye to my garden, and took my Shane with me, even though he had only months left on this earth, and it broke our hearts to separate, but there was no other answer, it had to be faced, or I would end in the darkness that I came from along with him.

He of course, was already there. I can see him, pacing the floor as if he was back in his cell, a place similar to his shell, where he felt most at home, yet a place that stifled him, left him stunted, unable to fulfil his potential. Without me there to pander to, to look after, he was able to retreat, from his friends, his family, from me, but not from himself. He lives in dark rooms, behind closed doors, and phones that endlessly ring without being answered.

2

So all these wrecks resume their shattered

lives; yet, at night, even now, centuries later, when

the eyes are closed, they still can see the double bars, illuminated by the ghostly lights of the yard; the mind wandering back through time, watching figures, like sad rag dolls slowly in dream sequence, crumbling to the floor in a red mist, a row of many insane faces with gaping mouths, twisting with screams, shouts, but in silence, the sound too numb to travel the time warp;

And then, in that cell, the stillness or the pain, taking human shape, and walking the worn floor, its steps beating rhythmically, faster and faster, like a bursting flooded heart, till darkness finally, mercifully, closes its curtain on the world of mice and men.

Here is a clever mouse in a cellar of midgets,

he sees the light under the door at the top

of the stairs,

but the space between the steps is too far to

reach,

and even if he could,

he is afraid of what he might find there

at the top of the stairs.

Walking through the dead leaves,

the last survivor of a centuries-old atomic

blast,

kicking the waste products of a machine-

like nature

under his feet.

he feels the hopelessness of primeval man

confronted by the ice age.

Waiting to wake from a dread sleep

with all its claustrophobia,

trying to tear the cobwebs from the walls

of this World,

and rid the earth of the never-dying worm

that burrows through the brain in never-

ending circles.

Why, there he goes now,

scuttling through his mousehole.

3

Even after all this time, we keep in
touch now and again, we share a Son after all. And
though we live far apart, and in ways neither
knows anything about, I will never forget those
times of sunshine as well as heartache, a learning
process that caused so much pain, and with it,
some kind of enlightenment. Perhaps if we both
had not been so damaged as people in our own

ways, we may have survived it better. Then again, without those lessons, would we be who we are now?

4

And as the redness recedes, can such a
journey be contemplated again? Knowing that
justice is only revenge, the sword not the scales;
knowing that it is wrong to make your way in the
world on someone else's back? Knowing that
those who sit at the head of the table are often
crooks who are never caught? Can such a journey
be contemplated again?

The system tends to be geared up for one kind of thought; in truth, the explorers are often eaten by the lions, the inventors fail to register the patents that the world makes such use of. Good thoughts are not the exclusive property of the educated. The boy at the top of the class may be excellent at English language, but a parrot can be taught to speak, and will not necessarily understand a word he is saying.

When dreams go sour, and the need is still great, problems begin. A vacuum is always filled; if ability does not feel rewarded, it will always find a way to give expression to itself; it must do this, or die, and all the floggings in the world will not change nature, or the spots on a leopard, they will merely leave a deep scar on the skin. No gold is sufficient to brighten the stigmata, but being sick at heart has no easy cure.

And as Wandsworth is left behind, perhaps it could be said that nothing has been gained from this experience but knowledge of man's inhumanity to man. The suffered desperately seeks justification to himself for this journey, but even the friendships gained, prove, in the end, to be still-born, created out of the terror in the trenches, certainly nothing that can be sustained in the larger world, promises, like lives, lying broken in the process.

A psychiatrist will say that a man who finds life hard to live because he has no illusions is actually seeing existence as it is; the cure is to convince the man to accept illusions again, so that he can complete his allotted time at peace with himself.

In the Wandsworths of this world, the need

for such illusions is strong; to confirm existence,

to react against impotence by seeming to convince

that power and influence can still be exercised,

even among the tadpoles of a murky pond.

Surrounded by awfulness, the dreams gathered

must be those of hope, however futile in the end.

Easy therefore to dismiss such dreams, and claim

that the black birds know best, drawn as they are

to the atmosphere that hangs like a pall over the

yard lights;

But if such dreams are illusion, bringing

comfort from the pain, then they are surely no

worse than pleasure, pure distraction, giving

nothing in return; and though such rewards may

not be forthcoming, perhaps forever in this life,

grief is growth, even to those who cannot see that

the soul must make its journey, despite the dreams

of the traveller.

These strands that bind us; five years

after Julie, Del dies

of the same sickness in the same season; it

is

less than two years since he left

to find freedom.

CPSIA information can be obtained
at www.ICGtesting.com
Printed in the USA
BVOW10*0142121016

464759BV00015B/2/P